D0205389

14. go on a Cruise

15. healing and divine health

16.

17.

18.

19.

20.

21.

22.

23.

24.

25.

26.

27.

28.

29.

30.

31.

# ☙ 2 ☙
# MY 12 MONTH GOALS

"...that I may *daily* perform my vows." (Psalm 61:8)

| | GOALS | DATE |
|---|---|---|
| 1. | Progress to Adult Branch | January |
| 2. | Working with Suns | February |
| 3. | | March |
| 4. | Join ISA - Savings | April |
| 5. | Financial Harvest | May |
| 6. | Lose weight | June |
| 7. | Purchase new car | July |
| 8. | Debt cancelled overdraft/catalogue | Aug |
| 9. | excell with 70+ marks Pass my Exams in unit 1+3 | Sept |
| 10. | | October |
| 11. | | Nov |
| 12. | | Dec |

# TABLE OF CONTENTS

CHAPTER

PAGE

*MY PERSONAL DREAM BOOK*
Copyright © 2001 by *DR. MIKE MURDOCK*　ISBN 1-56394-129-5
Published by The Wisdom Center
P.O. Box 99 • Denton, Texas 76202

# ☙ 1 ☙

# MY LIFETIME DREAMS
# & GOALS

"When Your Heart Chooses A Destination
Your Mind Will Create the Map To Reach It."
-*MIKE MURDOCK*

| GOALS (b) | DATE |
|---|---|
| 1. Financial Harvest-$1u | 2002 |
| 2. Siblings Savings - (C) | 2004 |
| 3. Pass my Nursing Diploma - A grades | 2002 |
| 4. Marry a man of God - (A) happy | |
| 5. Debt Cancellation - no more borrowing or waste | Dec 2006 |
| 6. Divine acceleration - parents to move home | June 2001 |
| 7. Travel around the world | |
| 8. Become diligent in the word | |
| 9. To buy my own house | |
| 10. Invest in Kingdom of God | |
| 11. To have children | |
| 12. To have a new car | |
| 13. To continue working with Swiss | |

# ❧ 3 ❧

# HOW TO TAKE NOTES

| TOPIC | THOUGHT |
|---|---|
| January 16, 2001<br>The Secret Place<br>*Numbers 23:19 | Memory Scripture Of The Day<br>"God is not a man, that He should lie; neither the son of man, that He should repent:  hath He said, and shall He not make it good?" |
| Ps. 123-150;<br>Proverbs. 1-12 | My 40 Chapters in the Word. |
| Law of the Seed<br>Law of the Harvest | "They that sow in tears shall reap in joy. He that goeth forth and weepeth, bearing precious seed, shall doubtless come again with rejoicing, bringing his sheaves with him" (Psalms 126:5-6). |
| Children | ...  are an heritage of the Lord.<br>...  are a reward from God to parents.<br>...  were intended to be a source of great joy.<br>(Ps. 127:3-5) (Ps. 128:3) |
| Job<br>Happiness | *Your job and career should be a source of great joy and provision.*<br>"For thou shalt eat the labour of thine hands: happy shalt thou be, and it shall be well with thee" (Psalms 128:2). |

| TOPIC | THOUGHT |
|---|---|
| 14 Facts About God | 1. God is righteous (Ps. 129:4).<br>2. God gives children as gifts to us (Psalms 127:3).<br>3. God gives a wife as a gift to the man who fears God (Psalms 128:3-4).<br>4. God loves doing great things for us (Psalms 126:2-3).<br>5. God is great (Psalms 125:5).<br>6. God is above every God (Ps. 135:5-6).<br>7. God can do anything He desires (Psalms 135:6-13).<br>8. God will judge His people (Psalms 135:14).<br>9. God's mercy endures forever (Psalms 136).<br>10. God is continually perfecting our lives (Psalms 138:8).<br>11. God always respects the humble (Psalms 138:6).<br>12. God surrounds us continually (Psalms 139:1-12).<br>13. God thinks about us constantly (Psalms 139:17-18).<br>14. God can turn failure into success (Psalms 145:14). |
| Prosperity | (Psalms 145:15:16) |
| Word of God | Everything created by God is used to fulfill and carry out His Word. "Fire, and hell; snow, and vapour; stormy wind fulfilling His Word" (Psalms 148:8). |

| TOPIC | THOUGHT |
|---|---|
| Wisdom | ... is the most important thing on earth (Proverbs 4:7). |
| Relationship | ... delivers us from wrong people (Proverbs 2:12,16). |
| | ... determines longevity (Pro. 3:2). |
| Favor | ... determines favor (Pro. 3:4). |
| | ... determines wealth (Pro. 3:16). |
| | ... creates peace (Proverbs 3:18). |
| | ... is the instrument of creativity used by God in creating the universe (Pro. 3:19). |
| | ... brings protection (Pro. 3:21-22). |
| | ... prevents backsliding (Pro. 3:23). |
| Health | ... affects our health (Pro. 3:24). |
| | ... removes fear (Pro. 3:24-25). |
| Promotion | ... is the key to promotion and honor (Proverbs 4:7-9). |
| | |
| Law of the Seed | *God commanded us to sow good seed in every person possible around us.* "Withhold not good from them to whom it is due, when it is in the power of thine hand to do it (Pro. 3:27). |
| | |
| Passion for the Word | (Proverbs 7:1-3) |
| | |
| Fear of the Lord | ... is the beginning of Wisdom and knowledge (Proverbs 9:10, 1:7). |

# ≈ 4 ≈
# 12 INGREDIENTS OF THE PERFECT DAY

"But the path of the just is as the shining light, that shineth more and more unto *The Perfect Day*." (Prov. 4:18)

1. **Preparation...**Of Your Mind, Spirit And Body.
2. **Meditation...**On The Law of God, Our Wisdom.
3. **Motivation...**The Stirring Up Of Passion And Enthusiasm For Your Assignment.
4. **Organization...**Of Daily Schedule Of Appointments.
5. **Elimination...**Of Any Appointment Or Request That Does Not Qualify For Your Focus.
6. **Delegation...**Of Tasks To Others.
7. **Impartation...**From Your Mentors And To Protégés.
8. **Vocation...**The Problem You Are Assigned To Solve.
9. **Information...**The Pursuit Of Wisdom And Knowledge.
10. **Celebration...**Of Family And Those You Love.
11. **Documentation...** Journal Of Your Daily Experiences.
12. **Restoration...**Of Health Through Exercise, And Sleep.

## YOUR DAILY SUCCESS ROUTINE

1. Perfect Your Daily Success Routine. The Secret Of Your Future Is Hidden In Your Daily Routine.
2. Set A Specific Prayer Time In Your Secret Place To Meet With The Holy Spirit.
3. Listen Continually For The Voice Of Your Mentor, The Holy Spirit.
4. Write Your Daily Goals Down Every Day.
5. Document And Visualize Your Dreams And Goals.
6. Always Keep 25% Of Your Day Unscheduled To Allow For Unexpected Interruptions.

# ❧ 5 ❧
# MY SCHEDULE & SUCCESS SHEET

| | *What I Plan To Happen!* | *What Happened!* |
|---|---|---|
| 7:00am | | |
| 8:00am | | |
| 9:00am | | |
| 10:00am | | |
| 11:00am | | |
| 12 noon | | |
| 1:00pm | | |
| 2:00pm | | |
| 3:00pm | | |
| 4:00pm | | |
| 5:00pm | | |
| 6:00pm | | |
| 7:00pm | | |
| 8:00pm | | |
| 9:00pm | | |
| 10:00pm | | |

# ⟋ 6 ⟍

# 31 DAYS TO
# ACHIEVING YOUR DREAM

1. Your Dream Is Anything You Want To *Become, Do* Or *Have* During Your Lifetime.

2. Your Dream Must Be *Believed, Pursued* And *Protected* To Be Achieved.

3. Your Dream Can Come True Regardless Of Your Personal Limitations.

4. Your Dream Should Always Determine What You Do *First* Each Morning.

5. The Dream You Are Pursuing Will Always Control And Dictate Your Daily Conduct And Behavior.

6. Your Daily Conversation Is A Portrait Of Your Passion For The Dream You Are Pursuing.

7. Every Daily *Appointment* Should Be A Stepping Stone Toward The Fulfillment Of Your Dream.

8. Your Dream May Birth Changes In Your Relationships.

9. Your Dream Will Determine Who Reaches For You.

10. Your Dream Should Be Born Within You, Not Borrowed From Others.

11. Your Dream May Require A Geographical Change.

12. Your Dream Determines Who Qualifies For Access.

13. Your Dream Should Qualify For Your Total Focus.

14. Your Dream Will Require Seasons Of Preparation.

15. Achieving Your Dream May Require An Uncommon Mentor.

16. Your Dream Is Your True Significant Difference From Another.

17. Satan Will Often Use Memories Of Your Past Failures To Distort The Dream God Is Developing In You.

18. Your Success Cannot Begin Until You Fuel Your Passion For The Dream Within You.

19. Your Family May Often Focus On Your Weaknesses Instead Of The Dream Growing Within You.

20. If You Neglect The Dream Within You, It Will Eventually Wither And Die.

21. Your Dream May Require Uncommon Faith.

22. Your Dream May Be Birthed From Uncommon Tragedies And Painful Memories.

23. Your Dream May Be Misunderstood By Those Closest To You.

24. Your Dream May Be So Great That It Makes You Feel Fearful, Inadequate Or Inferior.

25. Your Dream Is Your Invisible Companion Accompanying You From Your Present Into Your Future.

26. The Passion For Your Dream Must Increase So Strong That It Burns Within You Without The Encouragement Of Others.

27. Your Dream May Expose Adversarial Relationships In Your Life.

28. Your Dream Will Require Uncommon Favor From Others.

29. Every Relationship Will Move You Toward Your Dream Or Away From It.

30. When You Boldly Announce Your Dream, You Will Create An Instant Bond With Every Person Who Wanted To Accomplish The Same Dream.

31. You Must Practice Continual Visualization Of Your Dream.

# ☞ 7 ☞
# 31 FACTS YOU SHOULD
# KNOW ABOUT WISDOM

1.  Wisdom Is The Master Key To All The Treasures Of Life.
    (2 Chron. 1:7-8,10,11,12;Col. 2:2-3)

2.  Wisdom Is A Gift From God To You.
    (2 Sam. 2:3;Proverbs 2:6;Dan. 2:21;Eph. 2:17;1 Cor. 12:8)

3.  The Fear Of God Is The Beginning Of Wisdom.
    (Job 28:28;Ps. 111:10;Pro. 9:10)

4.  Jesus Is Made Unto Us Wisdom. (1 Cor. 1:30;Eph. 1:5,8,17)

5.  The Holy Spirit Is The Spirit Of Wisdom That Unleashes Your
    Gifts. (Ex. 31:1,3-4;Ex. 36:1b;Dan. 1:4)

6.  The Word Of God Is Able To Make You Wise Unto Salvation.
    (Ps. 107:43;John 5:39;2 Tim. 3:15)

7.  The Wisdom Of God Is Foolishness To The Natural Mind.
    (Pro. 18:2;Isa. 55:8-9;1 Cor. 2:4-5)

8.  Your Conversation Reveals How Much Wisdom You Possess.
    (I Kings 10:24;Pro. 18:21;Pro. 29:11;James 3:2)

9.  The Wisdom Of This World Is A False Substitute For The
    Wisdom Of God. (1 Cor. 2:4,13;James 3:13-17)

10. All The Treasures Of Wisdom And Knowledge Are Hid In
    Jesus Christ. (1 Cor. 1:23-24;1 Cor. 2:7-8;Col. 2:2-3)

11. The Word Of God Is Your Source Of Wisdom.
    (Deut. 4:5-6;Ps.119:98-100;Pro. 2:6)

12. God Will Give You Wisdom When You Take The Time To
    Listen. (Pro. 2:6;Isa. 40:31;John 10:27;James 1:5)

13. Right Relationships Increase Your Wisdom.
    (Pro. 13:20;1 Cor. 15:33;II Thes. 3:6;1 Tim. 6:5)

14. The Wisdom Of Man Is Foolishness To God.
    (1 Cor. 1:20-21,25;1 Cor. 3:19)

15. Men Of Wisdom Will Always Be Men Of Mercy. (Gal. 6:1;James 3:17;James 5:19-20)

16. Wisdom Is Better Than Jewels Or Money. (Job 28:18;Pro. 3:13-15;Pro. 8:11;Pro. 16:16)

17. Wisdom Is More Powerful Than Weapons Of War. (Pro.12:6;Eccl. 9:18;Isa. 33:6;Acts 6:10)

18. The Mantle Of Wisdom Makes You 10 Times Stronger Than Those Without It. (Ps. 91:7;Eccl. 7:19;Dan. 1:17,20)

19. The Wise Hate Evil...The Evil Hate The Wise. (Pro. 1:7,22;Pro. 8:13;Pro. 9:8;Pro. 18:2a)

20. Wisdom Reveals The Treasure In Yourself. (Pro. 19:8;Eph. 2:10;Phil. 1:6;1 Peter 2:9-10)

21. The Proof Of Wisdom Is The Presence Of Joy And Peace. (Ps. 119:165;Pro. 3:13;Eccl. 7:12;James 3:17)

22. Wisdom Makes Your Enemies Helpless Against You. (Pro. 16:7;Eccl. 7:12;Isa. 54:17;Luke 21:15)

23. Wisdom Creates Currents Of Favor And Recognition Toward You. (Pro. 3:1,4;Pro. 4:8;Pro. 8:34-35)

24. The Wise Welcome Correction. (Pro. 3:11-12;Pro.9:8-9)

25. When The Wise Speak, Healing Flows. (Pro. 10:11,20,21;Pro. 12:18)

26. When You Increase Your Wisdom, You Will Increase Your Wealth.   (Ps. 112:1,3;Pro. 3:16;Pro. 8:18,21;Pro. 14:24)

27. Wisdom Can Be Imparted By The Laying On Of Hands Of A Man Of God. (Deut. 34:9; Acts 6:6,8,10;2 Tim. 1:6,14)

28. Wisdom Guarantees Promotion. (Pro. 4:8-9; Pro. 8:15-16; Ez. 7:25)

29. Wisdom Loves Those Who Love Her. (Pro. 2:3-5; Pro. 8:17,21)

30. He That Wins Souls Is Wise. (Pro. 11:30;Dan. 12:3; Rom. 10:14-15)

31. Wisdom Will Be Given To You When You Pray For It In Faith.  (Matt. 7:78-8,11;James 1:5-6)

# ☙ 8 ☙

# 31 Days To Understanding Your Mentor, The Holy Spirit

1. The Holy Spirit Is A Person, Not A Dove, Wind Or Fire. (John 14:16)

2. The Holy Spirit Created You. (Job 33:4)

3. The Holy Spirit Is The Author Of All Scripture And The Inspiration Of All Scripture. (2 Timothy 3:16)

4. The Holy Spirit Confirms That Jesus Is Within You. (1 John 4:13)

5. The Holy Spirit Decides The Skills, Gifts And Talents Within You. (1 Corinthians 12:4-11)

6. The Holy Spirit Gives Life. (2 Corinthians 3:6)

7. The Holy Spirit Confirms You Are A Child Of God. (Rom. 8:16)

8. The Holy Spirit Imparts A Personal Prayer Language That Dramatically Increases Your Strength And Faith. (Ju. 1:20)

9. The Holy Spirit Talks To You. (Revelation 2:7)

10. The Holy Spirit Reveals The Truth You Need To Live Victoriously. (John 16:13)

11. The Holy Spirit Is The Source Of The Anointing... The Special Power Of God Given For Your Assignment. (Luke 4:18)

12. The Holy Spirit Is The Source Of Every Desired Emotion You Are Pursuing In Your Life. (Galatians 5:22-23)

13. The Holy Spirit Knows Every Detail Of The Purpose And Plan Of God For Your Life. (Romans 8:27-28)

14. The Holy Spirit Decides When You Are Ready To Be Tested. (Luke 4:1-2)

15. The Holy Spirit Is Your Intercessor On Earth. (Romans 8:26)

16. The Holy Spirit Loves Singing. (Psalms 100:1-2)

17. The Holy Spirit Is The Source Of Your Joy. (Psalms 16:11)

18. The Holy Spirit Raised Jesus From The Dead, And He Will Raise You From The Dead When Christ Returns To The Earth. (Romans 8:11)

19. The Holy Spirit Removes All Fear. (2 Timothy 1:7)

20. The Holy Spirit Shows You Pictures Of Your Future. (John 16:13; Acts 7:55)

21. The Holy Spirit Gives You The Necessary Love You Need Towards Others. (Romans 5:5)

22. The Holy Spirit Decides Your Assignment. (Acts 13:2-4)

23. The Holy Spirit Enables You To Enter Into The Kingdom Of God. (John 3:5-6)

24. The Holy Spirit Only Guides Those Who Are Sons Of God. (Romans 8:14)

25. The Holy Spirit Knows The Person To Whom You Have Been Assigned. (Acts 8:29)

26. The Holy Spirit Will Send Inner Warnings To Protect You From Wrong People And Places. (Acts 16:6-7)

27. The Holy Spirit Is Grieved And Saddened By Wrong Conduct. (Ephesians 4:30-31)

28. The Holy Spirit Critiques Every Moment, Motive, And Movement Of Your Life. (Jeremiah 17:10)

29. The Holy Spirit Becomes An Enemy To The Rebellious. (Isaiah 63:10)

30. The Holy Spirit Withdraws When Offended. (Ephesians 4:30-32; Hosea 5:15)

31. The Holy Spirit Raised Jesus From The Dead, And He Will Raise You From The Dead When Christ Returns To The Earth. (Romans 8:11)

# ☞ 9 ☜

# 31 DAYS TO UNDERSTANDING YOUR ASSIGNMENT

1.  Everything God Created Was Created To Solve A Problem.

2.  Your Assignment Is Always To A Person Or A People.

3.  Your Assignment Is Not Your Decision, But Your *Discovery*.

4.  What You Hate Is A Clue To Something You Are Assigned To *Correct*.

5.  What *Grieves* You Is A Clue To Something You Are Assigned To *Heal*.

6.  What You Love Is A Clue To The Gifts, Skills, And *Wisdom* You Contain.

7.  Your Assignment Is *Geographical*.

8.  Your Assignment Will Take You Where You Are *Celebrated* Instead Of Tolerated.

9.  Your Assignment Is Your Significant Difference From Others.

10. If You Rebel Against Your Assignment, God May Permit Painful Experiences To Correct You.

11. What You Love Most Is A Clue To Your Assignment.

12. God Can Forgive Any Sin Or Mistake You Have Made In Pursuit Of Your Assignment.

13. Your Assignment Will Require *Seasons Of Preparation*.

14. Your Assignment May Contain *Seasons Of Insignificance.*

15. Your Assignment May Require *Seasons Of Waiting.*

16. Your Assignment May Require *Seasons Of Isolation.*

17. You Are The Only One God Has Anointed For Your Specific Assignment.

18. People Will Be Assigned By Hell To Distract, Delay, Discourage, And Derail Your Assignment.

19. Your Assignment May Sometimes Seem To Be In Vain.

20. Your Assignment Will Require Miracles.

21. Your Assignment Will Require Your *Total Focus.*

22. You Must Only Attempt A God-Given And God-Approved Assignment.

23. You Will Only Succeed When Your Assignment Becomes An Obsession.

24. Your Assignment Requires *Planning.*

25. Your Assignment Will Be Revealed *Progressively.*

26. Intercessors Can Determine The Outcome Of Your Assignment.

27. Someone Is Always Observing You Who Is Capable Of Greatly Blessing You In Your Assignment.

28. Your Assignment May Require Unusual And Unwavering Trust In A Man Or Woman Of God.

29. The Problem That *Infuriates* You The Most Is Often The Problem God Has Assigned You To Solve.

30. Your Assignment May Seem Small, Yet Be The Golden Link In A Great Chain Of Miracles.

31. Your Assignment Is The Only Place Financial Provision Is Guaranteed.

# ☙ 10 ☙
# 31 Things God Wants To Increase In Your Life

1. God Wants To Increase *The Miracles* You Experience (Mk. 11:23-14).

2. God Wants To Increase *Your Revelation* Of The Holy Spirit In Your Life (Psalms 25:12-14, John 14,15,16).

3. God Wants To Increase *Your Wisdom* (Proverbs 4:7, James 1:5, Ephesians 1:8).

4. God Wants To Increase *Your Finances* (Psalms 112:1b,3).

5. God Wants To Increase *Your Life* Span On The Earth (Ephesians 6:2-3, Psalms 92:14).

6. God Wants To Increase *Your Love* For Others (1 John. 2:5, Romans 5:5).

7. God Wants To Increase *Your Joy* (John 15:11-12).

8. God Wants To Increase *The Fruit* You Produce (Col. 1:12).

9. God Wants *Your Strength* To Increase (Colossians 1:11).

10. God Wants To Increase The *Flow Of Blessings* Into Your Life (Deuteronomy 28:1-14).

11. God Wants To Increase *Your Victories* Over Your Enemies (Deuteronomy 28:7).

12. God Wants To Increase *Your Endurance* Ability (Acts 5:41).

13. God Wants To Increase *Your Peace* (Philippians 4:7).

14. God Wants To Increase *Your Gratitude And Thankfulness* Toward Him (1 Thessalonians 5:18).

15. God Wants To Increase *Your Intercession And Prayer Life* (1 Thessalonians 5:17).

16. God Wants To Increase *Your Healing And Health* (Isa. 58:8).

17. God Wants To Increase *Your Soulwinning* (Mark 16:15, Proverbs 11:30).

18. God Wants To Increase *The Flow Of Favor* Into Your Life (Psalms 5:12).

19. God Wants To Increase *The Laughter And Shouting* In Your Life (Psalms 98:4).

20. God Wants To Increase *The Protection* Around You (Ps. 91:10-11).

21. God Wants To Increase *Your Achievements* (Ephesians 3:20).

22. God Wants To Increase *His Power* In Your Life (Acts 1:8).

23. God Wants To Increase *Your Pleasure And Enjoyment* In His World (Psalms 36:8-9).

24. God Wants To Increase *Your Rest And Relaxation* (Ps. 37:7).

25. God Wants To Increase *The Fear Of God* In Your Life (Pr. 9:10).

26. God Wants To Increase *The Good You Are Doing* Toward Others (Proverbs 3:27).

27. God Wants To Increase *Your Self-Confidence* In Accomplishing Your Assignment (Proverbs 3:25-26).

28. God Wants To Increase *The Time You Spend In The Secret Place* With Him (Psalms 27:4).

29. God Wants To Increase *Your Integrity And Purity* (Ps. 25:21).

30. God Wants To Increase *The Forgiveness* You Sow Into Others (Luke 6:38).

31. God Wants To Increase *Your Sowing* So Your Reaping Can Increase (2 Corinthians 9:6).

# ☙ 11 ☙
# 31 FACTS ABOUT
# THE LAW OF THE SEED

1. There Will Never Be A Day In Your Life That You Have Nothing To Sow.

2. You Will Always Reap What You Sow.

3. Seed-Faith Is Sowing What You Have Been Given To Create What You Have Been Promised.

4. Your Seed Is Anything That Blesses Somebody.

5. The Law Of The Seed (Sowing And Reaping) Was Intended To Birth Encouragement, Hope And Excitement Toward A Harvest.

6. Your Seed Is Any Tool God Has Given You To Create Your Future.

7. Something You Have Been Given By God Will Create Anything Else You Have Been Promised By God.

8. You Are A Walking Collection Of Seeds.

9. Someone Near You Is "The Soil" Qualified To Receive Your Seed.

10. When You Let Go Of What Is In Your Hand, God Will Let Go Of What Is In His Hand.

11. Everything You Possess Is Something You Have Been Given.

12. If You Keep What You Presently Have, That Is The Most It Will Ever Be.

13. When You Ask God For A Harvest, God Will Always Ask You For A Seed.

14. Your Seed Is The Only Proof You Have Mastered Greed.

15. When You Increase The Size Of Your Seed, You Increase The Size Of Your Harvest.

16. A Seed Of Nothing Always Schedules A Season Of Nothing.

17. Your Seed Must Always Be Comparable To The Harvest You Are Desiring.

18. Every Seed Contains An Invisible Instruction.

19. Your Seed Is Always Your Door Out Of Trouble.

20. When You Give Your Seed An Assignment You Are Giving Your Faith An Instruction.

21. Nothing Leaves Heaven Until Something Leaves Earth.

22. Your *Seed* Is *What* God Multiplies; Your *Faith* Is *Why* He Multiplies It.

23. When You Sow Into Others What Nobody Else Is Willing To Sow, You Will Reap What No One Else Has Ever Reaped.

24. Your Seed Is The Only Influence You Have Over Your Future.

25. Your Seed Is The Only Master Your Future Will Obey.

26. The Seed Of Forgiveness Into Others Creates The Harvest Of Mercy From Others.

27. What You *Keep* Is Your Harvest; What You *Sow* Is Your Seed.

28. When God Talks To You About A Seed, He Has A Harvest On His Mind.

29. The Seed That Leaves Your Hand Never Leaves Your Life- It Just Leaves Your Hand And Enters Into Your Future Where It Multiplies.

30. Your Seed Is A Photograph Of Your Faith.

31. An Uncommon Seed Always Creates An Uncommon Harvest.

# ☞12☜
# 31 Wisdom Keys Of Mike Murdock

1. Never Complain About What You Permit.

2. When Your Heart Chooses A Destination, Your Mind Will Create The Map.

3. The Proof Of Desire Is Pursuit.

4. What You Respect You Will Attract.

5. The Secret Of Your Future Is Hidden In Your Daily Routine.

6. The Problem That Infuriates You The Most Is The Problem You Have Been Assigned To Solve.

7. The Size Of Your Enemy Determines The Size Of Your Reward.

8. What You Make Happen For Others God Will Make Happen For You.

9. If You Insist On Taking What God Did Not Give You, God Will Take Back What He Gave You.

10. An Uncommon Seed Always Creates An Uncommon Harvest.

11. What You Can Tolerate You Cannot Change.

12. Any Movement Toward Order Will Expose What Does Not Belong In Your Life.

13. Your Rewards In Life Are Determined By The Problems You Solve.

14. The Atmosphere You Create Determines The Product You Produce.

15. What You See Determines What You Desire.

16. Your Respect For Time Is A Prediction Of Your Financial Future.

17. God Never Responds To Pain, But Always Responds To Pursuit.

18. Greatness Is Not The Absence Of A Flaw, But The Survival Of Your Flaw.

19. One Day Of Favor Is Worth A Thousand Days Of Labor.

20. The Anointing You Respect Is The Anointing You Attract.

21. Those Who Sin With You Eventually Sin Against You.

22. When You Want Something You've Never Had, You've Got To Do Something You've Never Done.

23. The Proof Of Love Is The Investment Of Time.

24. What You Are Willing To Walk Away From Determines What God Will Bring To You. *Ruth left moabto ge Boa3*

25. What You Fail To Destroy Will Eventually Destroy You.

26. What You Hear Determines What You See.

27. What You Love Will Reward You.

28. What You Permit To Enter Your Life Will Determine What Exits Your Life.

29. What You Repeatedly Hear You Will Eventually Believe.

30. What You Have In Your Hand Will Create Whatever You Want In Your Future.

31. False Accusation Is The Last Stage Before Supernatural Promotion.

# ⚬13⚬

# THE COVENANT OF 58 BLESSINGS

1. **Abilities** — Ex. 31:3; Rom. 12:6; 1 Cor. 12:4-7
2. **Abundance** — Deut. 15:6-7; Deut. 30:9; Ps. 92:12
3. **Angels** — Ps. 34:7; Ps. 91:11-12; Isa. 63:9
4, **Assurance** — Gen. 26:3; Ezek. 34:16; John 14:18
5. **Authority** — Gen 1:27-28; Gen. 9:2; 2 Sam. 2:30
6. **Church** — Ps. 122:1; Isa. 54:17; Hag. 2:9; Rom. 12:5
7. **Confidence** — Isa. 40:31; 2 Cor. 3:5; 2 Cor. 9:8
8. **Deliverance** — Ex. 3:8; 2 Kings 17:39; Ps. 18:19
9. **Eternal Life** — Job 19:25-26; Matt. 16:25,27
10. **Eternal Honor** — Mal. 3:17; James 1:12; 1 Pet. 1:4
11. **Faith** — Luke 17:6; Rorn. 1:17; Rom. 5:1-2
12. **Faithfulness Of God** — Num. 23:19; 1 Kings 8:56
13. **Family** — Gen. 15:4-5; Gen. 22:17-18; Gen. 28:14
14. **Favor** — Gen. 12:2; Ps. 5:12; Ps. 30:5,7; Prov. 3:4
15. **Fellowship With God** — Deut. 31:8; Prov. 1:33
16. **Forgiveness** — Ps. 130:3-4; Isa. 43:25; Matt. 6:14
17. **Freedom From Fear** — Ps. 46:1-2; Ps. 56:3-4,9
18. **Freedom From Worry** — Ps. 3:5-6; Ps. 55:12
19. **Friendship** — Prov. 17:17; Prov. 18:24; Prov. 27:10
20. **Fruitfulness** — Deut. 28:4; Ps. 1:3; Ps. 92:14
21. **Grace** — Ps. 103:12-14; Isa. 53:5; Rom. 5:20
22. **Guidance** — Ps. 25:9; Ps. 32:8; Ps. 73:23-25
23. **Happiness** — Ps. 37:4-5; Ps. 63:4-5; Ps. 64:10
24. **Health** — Ex. 15:26; Ps. 103:2-3; Ps. 147:3; Jer. 30:17
25. **Heaven** — Dan. 12:3; Mark 14:25; John 14:2

26. **Holy Spirit** — Luke 11:13; John 7:38; John 14:26
27. **Hope** — Ps. 71:5; Ps. 119:49,81; Rom. 5:4-5
28. **Inspiration** — Job 32:8; Ps. 119:92,105; Prov. 20:27
29. **Intercession** — Isa. 53:12; Mark 11:24; Luke 18:1
30. **Joy** — Neh. 8:10; Ps. 3:3; Ps. 16:11; Ps. 30:5
31. **Justice** — Job 8:3; Job 37:23; Ps. 72:4; Ps. 89:14
32. **Knowledge** — 2 Chron. 1:12; Job 36:4b; Ps. 94:10
33. **Longevity** — Deut. 4:40; Deut. 11:21; Ps. 21:4
34. **Love** — John 3:16; John 15:10,12; Rom. 5:8
35. **Marriage** — Gen. 2:24; Ps. 128:3; Prov. 18:22
36. **Mercy** — Gen. 9:16; Gen. 39:21; Ex. 33:19
37. **Miracles** — Ex. 14:27-30; Ps. 105:39-40; Matt. 19:26
38. **Ministry** — Isa. 61:1; Matt. 22:14; John 15:16
39. **Peace** — Lev. 26:6; Ps. 29:11; Ps. 72:7; Isa. 26:3
40. **Power** — Ex. 9:16; Deut. 4:37; Deut. 11:25; Isa. 59:19
41. **Promotion** — Deut 28:13; 1 Sam. 2:8; Ps. 71:21
42. **Prosperity** — Gen. 13:14-15; Lev. 20:24; Lev. 26:9
43. **Protection** — Deut. 1:30; 2 Chron. 20:15; Ps. 91:2-7
44. **Provision** — Deut. 8:7-9; Deut. 28:3:5; 1 Kings 17:14
45. **Rest** — Ps. 4:8; Ps. 23:2; Prov. 1:33; Prov. 3:24
46. **Restoration** —Job 42:10; Ps. 23:3; Ps. 40:2-3
47. **Resurrection** — Isa. 25:8; John 5:21; John 11:25-26
48. **Riches** — Deut. 8:18; 1 Chron. 29:12; Prov. 8:18-19
49. **Salvation** — Ps. 27:1; Ps. 55:16; John 6:54; Rom. 1:16
50. **Security** — Ps. 26:1; Ps. 57:3; Ps. 62:2,7; Ps. 105:14-15
51. **Strength** — Josh. 23:9; 1 Chron. 16:27; Ps. 18:2,29,32
52. **Success** — Josh. 1:5,7-8; Ps. 112:1-2; Isa. 58:11
53. **Truth** — Num. 23:19; Ps. 91:4b; Mark 4:22
54. **Understanding** — I Kings 3:12; Ps. 111:10; Ps. 119:130
55. **Victory** — Ps. 60:12; Ps. 108:13; 1 Cor. 15:55-57
56. **Wisdom** — I Kings 4:29; Prov. 2:6-7; Luke 21:15
57. **Word Of God** — Ps. 1:2; Ps. 19:7-8; Ps. 107:20
58. **Work** — Ex. 23:12; Deut. 15:10; Deut. 28:2,12; Ps. 1:3

# ☞14☜
# ONE YEAR BIBLE READING SCHEDULE

**January**
1. Gen. 1-3
2. Gen. 4-6
3. Gen. 7-9
4. Gen. 10-14
5. Gen. 15-17
6. Gen. 18-20
7. Gen. 21-23
8. Gen. 24-26
9. Gen. 27-29
10. Gen. 30-32
11. Gen. 33-37
12. Gen. 38-40
13. Gen. 41-43
14. Gen. 44-46
15. Gen. 47-49
16. Gen. 50- Ex.1-2
17. Ex. 3-5
18. Ex. 6-10
19. Ex. 11-13
20. Ex. 14-16
21. Ex. 17-19
22. Ex. 20-22
23. Ex. 23-25
24. Ex. 26-28
25. Ex. 29-33
26. Ex. 34-36
27. Ex. 37-39
28. Ex. 40-Lev. 1-2
29. Lev. 3-5
30. Lev. 6-8
31. Lev. 9-11

**February**
1. Lev. 12-16
2. Lev. 17-19
3. Lev. 20-22
4. Lev. 23-25
5. Lev. 26-27- Num. 1
6. Num. 2-4
7. Num. 5-7
8. Num. 8-12
9. Num. 13-15
10. Num. 16-18
11. Num. 19-21
12. Num. 22-24
13. Num. 25-27
14. Num. 28-30
15. Num. 31-35
16. Num. 36-Dt. 1-2
17. Dt. 3-5
18. Dt. 6-8
19. Dt. 9-11
20. Dt. 12-14
21. Dt. 15-17
22. Dt. 18-22
23. Dt. 23-25
24. Dt. 26-28
25. Dt. 29-31
26. Dt. 32-34
27. Josh. 1-3
28. Josh. 4-6

**March**
1. Josh. 7-11
2. Josh. 12-14
3. Josh. 15-17
4. Josh. 18-20
5. Josh. 21-23
6. Josh. 24-Jud. 1-2
7. Jud. 3-5
8. Jud. 6-10
9. Jud. 11-13
10. Jud. 14-16
11. Jud. 17-19
12. Jud. 20-21 - Ruth 1
13. Ruth 2-4
14. 1 Sam. 1-3
15. 1 Sam. 4-8
16. 1 Sam. 9-11
17. 1 Sam. 12-14
18. 1 Sam. 15-17
19. 1 Sam. 18-20
20. 1 Sam. 21-23
21. 1 Sam. 24-26
22. 1 Sam. 27-31
23. 2 Sam. 1-3
24. 2 Sam. 4-6
25. 2 Sam. 7-9
26. 2 Sam. 10-12
27. 2 Sam. 13-15
28. 2 Sam. 16-18
29. 2 Sam. 19-23
30. 2 Sam. 24 - 1Ki. 1-2
31. 1 Ki. 3-5

**April**
1. 1 Ki. 6-8
2. 1 Ki. 9-11
3. 1 Ki. 12-14
4. 1 Ki. 15-17
5. 1 Ki. 18-22
6. 2 Ki. 1-3
7. 2 Ki. 4-6
8. 2 Ki. 7-9
9. 2 Ki. 10-12
10. 2 Ki. 13-15
11. 2 Ki. 16-18
12. 2 Ki. 19-23
13. 2 Ki. 24-25- 1 Chr. 1
14. 1 Chr. 2-4
15. 1 Chr. 5-7
16. 1 Chr. 8-10
17. 1 Chr. 11-13
18. 1 Chr. 14-16
19. 1 Chr. 17-21

20. 1 Chr. 22-24
21. 1 Chr. 25-27
22. 1 Chr. 28-29 -
    2 Chr. 1
23. 2 Chr. 2-4
24. 2 Chr. 5-7
25. 2 Chr. 8-10
26. 2 Chr. 11-15
27. 2 Chr. 16-18
28. 2 Chr. 19-21
29. 2 Chr. 22-24
30. 2 Chr. 25-27

**May**
1. 2 Chr. 28-30
2. 2 Chr. 31-33
3. 2 Chr. 34-36 -
   Ez. 1-2
4. Ez. 3-5
5. Ez. 6-8
6. Ez. 9-10 -
   Neh. 1
7. Neh. 2-4
8. Neh. 5-7
9. Neh. 8-10
10. Neh. 11-13 -
    Est. 1-2
11. Est. 3-5
12. Est. 6-8
13. Est. 9-10 -
    Job 1
14. Job 2-4
15. Job 5-7
16. Job 8-10
17. Job 11-15
18. Job 16-18
19. Job 19-21
20. Job 22-24
21. Job 25-27
22. Job 28-30
23. Job 31-33
24. Job 34-38
25. Job 39-41
26. Job 42 -
    Ps. 1-2
27. Ps. 3-5
28. Ps. 6-8
29. Ps. 9-11
30. Ps. 12-14
31. Ps. 15-19

**June**
1. Ps. 20-22
2. Ps. 23-25
3. Ps. 26-28
4. Ps. 29-31
5. Ps. 32-34
6. Ps. 35-37
7. Ps. 38-42
8. Ps. 43-45
9. Ps. 46-48
10. Ps. 49-51
11. Ps. 52-54
12. Ps. 55-57
13. Ps. 58-60
14. Ps. 61-65
15. Ps. 66-68
16. Ps. 69-71
17. Ps. 72-74
18. Ps. 75-77
19. Ps. 78-80
20. Ps. 81-83
21. Ps. 84-88
22. Ps. 89-91
23. Ps. 92-94
24. Ps. 95-97
25. Ps. 98-100
26. Ps. 101-103
27. Ps. 104-106
28. Ps. 107-111
29. Ps. 112-114
30. Ps. 115-117

**July**
1. Ps. 118-120
2. Ps. 121-123
3. Ps. 124-126
4. Ps. 127-129
5. Ps. 130-134
6. Ps. 135-137
7. Ps. 138-140
8. Ps. 141-143
9. Ps. 144-146
10. Ps. 147-149
11. Ps. 150 -
    Pro. 1-2
12. Pro. 3-7
13. Pro. 8-10
14. Pro. 11-13
15. Pro. 14-16
16. Pro. 17-19
17. Pro. 20-22

18. Pro. 23-25
19. Pro. 26-30
20. Pro. 31-Ecc. 1-2
21. Ecc. 3-5
22. Ecc. 6-8
23. Ecc. 9-11
24. Ecc. 12-SoS. 1-2
25. SoS. 3-5
26. SoS. 6-8-Is. 1-2
27. Is. 3-5
28. Is. 6-8
29. Is. 9-11
30. Is. 12-14
31. Is. 15-17

**August**
1. Is. 18-20
2. Is. 21-25
3. Is. 26-28
4. Is. 29-31
5. Is. 32-34
6. Is. 35-37
7. Is. 38-40
8. Is. 41-43
9. Is. 44-48
10. Is. 49-51
11. Is. 52-54
12. Is. 55-57
13. Is. 58-60
14. Is. 61-63
15. Is. 64-66
16. Jer. 1-5
17. Jer. 6-8
18. Jer. 9-11
19. Jer. 12-14
20. Jer. 15-17
21. Jer. 18-20
22. Jer. 21-23
23. Jer. 24-28
24. Jer. 29-31
25. Jer. 32-34
26. Jer. 35-37
27. Jer. 38-40
28. Jer. 41-43
29. Jer. 44-46
30. Jer. 47-51
31. Jer. 52-Lam. 1-2

**September**
1. Lam. 3-5
2. Ez. 1-3
3. Ez. 4-6

4. Ez. 7-9
5. Ez. 10-12
6. Ez. 13-17
7. Ez. 18-20
8. Ez. 21-23
9. Ez. 24-26
10. Ez. 27-29
11. Ez. 30-32
12. Ez. 33-35
13. Ez. 36-40
14. Ez. 41-43
15. Ez. 44-46
16. Ez. 47-48 - Dan. 1
17. Dan. 2-4
18. Dan. 5-7
19. Dan. 8-10
20. Dan. 11-12 - Hos. 1-3
21. Hos. 4-6
22. Hos. 7-9
23. Hos. 10-12
24. Hos. 13-14 - Joel 1
25. Jo. 2-3 - Amos. 1
26. Amos. 2-4
27. Amos. 5-9
28. Ob. 1 - Jon. 1-2
29. Jon. 3-4 - Mi. 1
30. Mi. 2-4

**October**
1. Mi. 5-7
2. Na. 1-3
3. Hab. 1-3
4. Zeph. 1-3- Hag. 1-2
5. Zechariah 1-3
6. Zech. 4-6
7. Zech. 7-9
8. Zech. 10-12
9. Zech. 13-14 - Mal. 1
10. Mal. 2-3
11. Matt. 1-5
12. Matt. 6-8
13. Matt. 9-11
14. Matt. 12-14
15. Matt. 15-17
16. Matt. 18-20
17. Matt. 21-23

18. Matt. 24-28
19. Mk. 1-3
20. Mk. 4-6
21. Mk. 7-9
22. Mk. 10-12
23. Mk. 13-15
24. Mk. 16-Lk. 1-2
25. Lk. 3-7
26. Lk. 8-10
27. Lk. 11-13
28. Lk. 14-16
29. Lk. 17-19
30. Lk. 20-22
31. Lk. 23-24-Jn. 1

**November**
1. Jn. 2-6
2. Jn. 7-9
3. Jn. 10-12
4. Jn. 13-15
5. Jn. 16-18
6. Jn. 19-21
7. Acts 1-3
8. Acts 4-8
9. Acts 9-11
10. Acts 12-14
11. Acts 15-17
12. Acts 18-20
13. Acts 21-23
14. Acts 24-26
15. Acts 27-28 - Rom. 1-3
16. Rom. 4-6
17. Rom. 7-9
18. Rom. 10-12
19. Rom. 13-15
20. Rom. 16 - 1 Cor. 1-2
21. 1 Cor. 3-5
22. 1 Cor. 6-10
23. 1 Cor. 11-13
24. 1 Cor. 14-16
25. 2 Cor. 1-3
26. 2 Cor. 4-6
27. 2 Cor. 7-9
28. 2 Cor. 10-12
29. 2 Cor. 13 - Gal. 1-4
30. Gal. 5-6 - Eph. 1

**December**
1. Eph. 2-4
2. Eph. 5-6 - Ph. 1
3. Ph. 2-4
4. Col. 1-3
5. Col. 4 - 1 Thes. 1-2
6. 1 Thes. 3-5 2 Thes. 1-2
7. 2 Thes. 3 1 Tim. 1-2
8. 1 Tim. 3-5
9. 1 Tim. 6 2 Tim. 1-2
10. 2 Tim. 3-4 - Ti. 1
11. Titus 2-3 - Phil. 1
12. Heb. 1-3
13. Heb. 4-8
14. Heb. 9-11
15. Heb. 12-13 James 1
16. James 2-4
17. James 5 1 Peter 1-2
18. 1 Peter 3-5
19. 2 Peter 1-3
20. 1 John 1-5
21. 2 John 1 3 John 1- Jude 1
22. Rev. 1-3
23. Rev. 4-5
24. Rev. 6-7
25. Rev. 8-9
26. Rev. 10-11
27. Rev. 12-16
28. Rev. 17-18
29. Rev. 19-20
30. Rev. 21-22
31. Well Done!

"Wisdom is the principal thing." Pro. 4:6

"This is your Wisdom and your Understanding." Deut. 4:6

# ⚚15⚚

# READING THE BIBLE
# THROUGH IN ONE MONTH

1. Gen. 1-40
2. Gen. 41-50 / Ex.1-30
3. Ex. 31-40 / Lev. 1-27 / Num. 1-3
4. Num. 4-36 / Deut. 1-7
5. Deut. 8-34 / Josh. 1-13
6. Josh. 14-24 / Jud. 1-21/ Ruth 1-4 / 1 Sam. 1-4
7. 1 Sam. 5-31 / 2 Sam. 1-13
8. 2 Sam. 14-24 / 1 Ki. 1-22 / 2 Ki. 1-7
9. 2 Ki. 8-25 / 1 Chron. 1-22
10. 1 Chron. 23-29 / 2 Chron. 1-33
11. 2 Chron. 34-36 / Ezra 1-10 / Neh. 1-13/ Est. 1-10 / Job 1-4
12. Job 5-42 / Ps. 1-2
13. Ps. 3-42
14. Ps. 43-82
15. Ps. 83-122
16. Ps. 123-150 / Prov. 1-12
17. Prov. 13-31 / Eccl. 1-12/ Song 1-8 / Isa. 1
18. Isa. 2-41
19. Ps. 42-66 / Jer. 1-15
20. Jer. 16-52 / Lam. 1-3
21. Lam. 4-5 / Ez. 1-40
22. Ez. 41-48 / Dan. 1-12 / Hos. 1-14 / Joel 1-3 / Amos 1-3
23. Amos 4-9 / Obadiah 1 / Jonah 1-4 / Micah 1-7 / Nahum 1-3 / Hab. 1-3 / Zeph. 1-3 / Hag. 1-2 / Zech. 1-14 / Mal. 1-4
24. Matt. 1-28 / Mark 1-12
25. Mark 13-16 / Luke 1-24 / John 1-12
26. John 13-21 / Acts 1-28 / Rom. 1-3
27. Rom. 4-16 / 1 Cor. 1-16 / 2 Cor. 1-11
28. 2 Cor. 12-13 / Gal.1-6 / Eph. 1-6 / Phil. 1-4 / Col. 1-4 / 1 Thes. 1-5 / 2 Thes. 1-3 / 1 Tim. 1-6 / 2 Tim. 1-4
29. Titus 1-3 / Philemon 1 / Heb. 1-13 / James 1-5 / 1 Pet. 1-5 / 2 Pet. 1-3 / 1 John 1-5 / 2 John 1 / 3 John 1 / Jude 1
30. Rev. 1-22

# MY PERSONAL LETTER TO YOU

## My Dear Friend,

*Your letter is very important to me.* You are a special person, and I believe that you are special to God. I want to assist you in any way possible. Write me when you need an intercessor to pray for you.

When you write, my staff and I will pray over your letter. I will write you back to help you receive the miracle you need.

*God has brought us together.*

*Will you become a monthly Faith Partner with my ministry?* Your Seeds are so powerful in helping heal broken lives. When you sow into the work of God, four Miracle Harvests are guaranteed in Scripture:

▶ Uncommon Protection (Mal. 3:10-11)
▶ Uncommon Favor (Lk. 6:38)
▶ Uncommon Health (Isa. 58:8)
▶ Uncommon Financial Ideas and Wisdom (Deut. 8:18)

Sow your Uncommon Seed today, then focus your expectations for the 100-fold return! (Mk. 10:28-30) An Uncommon Seed Will Always Create An Uncommon Harvest.

*I will look forward to your letter.*

# DECISION

## Will You Accept Jesus As Your Personal Savior Today?

The Bible says, "That if thou shalt confess with thy mouth the Lord Jesus, and shall believe in thine heart that God hath raised Him from the dead, thou shalt be saved." (Rom.10:9-10) Pray this prayer from your heart today!

*"Dear Jesus, I believe that you died for me and rose again on the third day. I confess I am a sinner... I need Your love and forgiveness...Come into my heart. Forgive my sins. I receive Your eternal life. Confirm Your love by giving me peace, joy and supernatural love for others."*
*Amen.*

# DR. MIKE MURDOCK

is in tremendous demand as one of the most dynamic speakers in America today.

More than 15,000 audiences in 38 countries have attended his meetings and seminars. Hundreds of invitations come to him from churches, colleges, and business corporations. He is a noted author of over 115 books, including the best sellers, *"The Leadership Secrets of Jesus"* and *"Secrets of the Richest Man Who Ever Lived"*. Thousands view his weekly television program, *"Wisdom Keys with Mike Murdock"*. Many have attended his annual School of Wisdom at his headquarters, *The Wisdom Center*, in Denton, Texas.

---

☐ Yes, Mike! I made a decision to accept Christ as my personal Savior today. Please send me my free gift of your book *"31 Keys to a New Beginning"* to help me with my new life in Christ. *(B48)*

NAME

ADDRESS

CITY                                        STATE   ZIP

PHONE                                       BIRTHDAY

E-MAIL

---

*Mail form to:*
**The Wisdom Center** • P.O. Box 99 • Denton, TX 76202
*Phone 940-891-1400 • Fax 940-891-4500 • www.mikemurdock.com*

# THE WISDOM 7
## WISDOM BOOK LIBRARY

# Your Search Is Over.

- ▶ 9 Keys In Making Your Time Count...p.35-36

- ▶ 4 Rewards of Pain..p.39

- ▶ 14 Seasons In A Minister's Life...p.49-50

- ▶ 15 Rewards For Completing Your Assignment...p.80-83

- ▶ The Benefits of Crisis...p.91

- ▶ 12 Keys That Unlock The Flow Of Miracles...p.91-94

- ▶ 7 Important Keys In Planning...p.121-122

- ▶ Importance Of Anger...p.155-158

*...and much more!*

Everything that God created was created to solve a problem. The key to successful living is discovering the purpose for which you were created. This is your "Assignment." This Volume I on "The Dream & The Destiny" will unleash in you the discovery of our life calling. You will begin to know the joy of being in the center of God's will for your life!

*Available also on six tapes for only $30!*

Wisdom Is The Principal Thing
B-74
$10
6 Cassettes for $30
TS22
The Wisdom Center

Order Today @ 1-800-WISDOM-1
The Wisdom Center • P.O. Box 99 • Denton, Texas • 76202
940-891-1400 • Fax: 940-891-4500 • www.mikemurdock.com

# The 500 Billion Dollar Mar

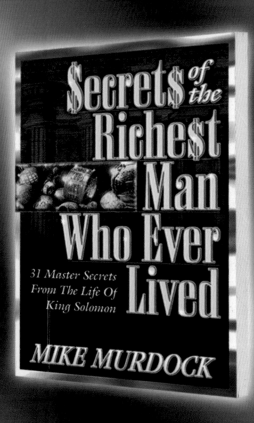

▶ 10 Important Facts You Should Recognize Abou Your Personal Limitations...p.25-30

▶ 10 Qualities of Uncommon Achievers...p.37-41

▶ 7 Keys To Help You Get Along With Others...p.5(

▶ 7 Immediate Steps You Take To Organize Your Dreams...p.62-63

▶ 9 Negotiation Keys Tha Will Help Anyone Get W They Want...p.70-72

▶ 7 Facts About Excellence That Could Change Your L Forever...p.84-86

▶ The Most Important Skill A Manager Can Possess...p.8

*...and muc mor*

**L**earning the secrets of great leaders should be a life-time study. Dr. Murdock has invested hundreds of hours studying the life principles of the most successful individuals in the world from past to present. This teaching on the life of Solomon will bring you to a high-er level of understanding in the secrets of uncommon wealth and success. God's best will soon be yours as you learn and put into practice these keys from the Richest Man Who Ever Lived!

*Available also on six tapes for only $30!*

Wisdom Is The Principal Thing
B-99
**$10**
6 Cassettes for $30
TS70
The Wisdom Center

**Order Today @ 1-800-WISDOM-1**
**The Wisdom Center • P.O. Box 99 • Denton, Texas • 76202**
940-891-1400 • Fax: 940-891-4500 • www.mikemurdock.com

# You Can Have It.

▶ Why Sickness Is Not The Will of God…p.10

▶ How To Release The Powerful Forces That Guarantees Blessing…p.19

▶ The Incredible Role Of Your Memory & The Imagination…p.41

▶ The Hidden Power Of Imagination & How To Use It Properly…p.41

▶ The Difference Between The Love Of God And His Blessings…p.8

▶ 3 Steps In Increasing Your Faith…p.83

▶ 2 Rewards That come When You Use Your Faith In God…p.13

▶ 7 Powerful Keys Concerning Your Faith…p.78

*…and much more!*

emands and desires as photographs within our hearts and minds - things that we want to happen our future. God plants these pictures as invisible eds within us. God begins every miracle in your life h a Seed-picture…the invisible idea that gives birth a visible blessing. In this teaching, you will discover r desires and how to concentrate on watering and rturing the growth of your Dream-Seeds until you ain your God-given goals.

*vailable also on six tapes for only $30!*

Wisdom Is The Principal Thing
B-11
**$9**
6 Cassettes for $30
TS2
The Wisdom Center

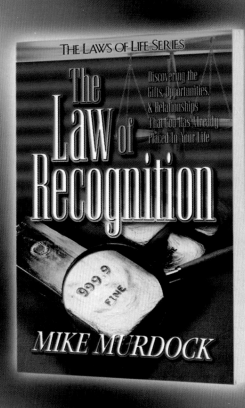

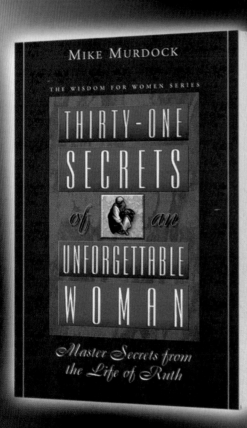

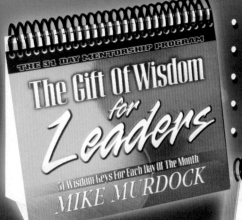

# WISDOM COLLECTION

# 8

# ECRETS OF THE UNCOMMON MILLIONAIRE

The Uncommon Millionaire Conference Vol. 1 (Six Cassettes)
The Uncommon Millionaire Conference Vol. 2 (Six Cassettes)
The Uncommon Millionaire Conference Vol. 3 (Six Cassettes)
The Uncommon Millionaire Conference Vol. 4 (Six Cassettes)
31 Reasons People Do Not Receive Their
Financial Harvest (256 Page Book)
Secrets of the Richest Man Who Ever Lived
(178 Page Book)
12 Seeds of Wisdom Books On 12 Topics
The Gift of Wisdom for Leaders Desk Calendar
Songs From The Secret Place (Music Cassette)
In Honor of the Holy Spirit (Music Cassette)
365 Memorization Scriptures On The Word Of God (Audio Cassette)

Wisdom Is The Principal Thing
**Gift of Appreciation**
**For Any Seed of**
**$200**
Or More To Our Ministry
The Wisdom Center

# WISDOM COLLECTION

## 1

## The Greatest Secret of the Universe

*Collection Includes:*

1. The Greatest Secret of the Universe (Six Cassettes)
2. The Holy Spirit Handbook (Six Cassettes)
3. Songs From the Secret Place (Six Music Cassettes)
4. The Holy Spirit—The Greatest Secret of the Universe (Video)
5. The Jesus Book (173 Page Book)
6. The Holy Spirit Handbook (166 Page Book)
7. 12 Seeds of Wisdom Books On 12 Topics
8. The Gift of Wisdom for Champions Desk Calendar
9. In Honor of the Holy Spirit (Music Cassette)
10. The Mentor's Manna—The Secret Place (Audio Cassette)
11. 365 Memorization Scriptures On The Word Of God (Audio Cassette)

Wisdom Is The Principal

**Gift of Appreciation
For Any Seed of
$200**
Or More To Our Ministry

**Order Today @ 1-800-WISDOM-1**
**The Wisdom Center • P.O. Box 99 • Denton, Texas • 76202**
**940-891-1400 • Fax: 940-891-4500 • www.mikemurdock.com**

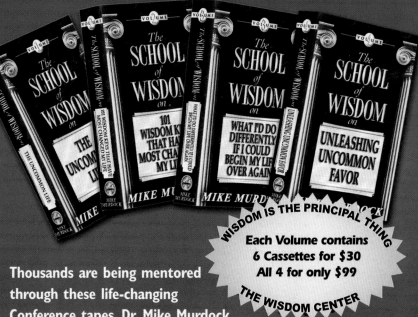

# WISDOM KEYS FOR AN UNCOMMON MINISTRY.